An Intimate Note to the Sincere Seeker

SRI SRI
RAVI SHANKAR

VOLUME 5: August 4, 1999 – July 19, 2000

ART OF LIVING FOUNDATION

An Intimate Note to the Sincere Seeker
Weekly Knowledge from Sri Sri Ravi Shankar
VOLUME 5: August 4, 1999 – July 19, 2000

Published by
Art of Living Foundation
Post Office Box 50003
Santa Barbara, California 93150
(877) 399-1008 (U.S. toll free)
(805) 564-1002
Printed in the United States of America

ISBN 1-885289-38-3

Compiled by Anne Elixhauser and Bill Hayden
Cover Design and Art Work: Bill Herman
Editorial Review: Laura Weinberg
Manuscript Preparation: Dmitri Potemkin

Message for the New Millennium

The sun rises and celebrates
The sky embraces and celebrates

Winds blow and celebrate
Rivers flow and celebrate

Birds sing and celebrate
Peacocks dance and celebrate

Trees flower and celebrate
Buds bloom and celebrate

We smile and serve
Meditate and celebrate

- Sri Sri Ravi Shankar

Jai Guru Dev

OTHER WORKS BY THE AUTHOR

Wisdom for the New Millennium
God Loves Fun
Waves of Beauty
Bang on the Door

Talks published singly:

The Language of the Heart
Prayer, the Call of the Soul
The Way Back Home
You Are the Blue Sky

The teachings of Sri Sri Ravi Shankar are available in
the form of books, video recordings and audiotapes.
For a catalog of products and to order,
contact:
Art of Living Books and Tapes
(800) 574-3001 U.S.A. or (641) 472-9892
Fax: (641) 472-0671
E-mail: aolmailorder@lisco.com

*Here in your hands
is the fifth treasure book
of intimate notes from*
Sri Sri Ravi Shankar
- a gift of wisdom and grace

Introduction

In June of 1995, Sri Sri Ravi Shankar began a weekly tradition of creating a short talk on a subject that was relevant to current events or to the collective minds of those who walked his path. These talks have been collected each year into volumes and made available to the whole world. Not only do people feel that the current Weekly Knowledge - as we call these intimate notes - applies to an immediate need, but there have been many instances where someone seeking wisdom or advice, picked up a volume and opened it randomly to find exactly what was required at that moment. The paradigm of time, space and separateness breaks down.

The knowledge is always fresh and extemporaneous. Those who are lucky enough to be with Guruji when the knowledge is created, find that the discussion brings forth truths that fill both the heart and the intellect. In the words of Guruji, "Being with the Guru means spontaneous integration of life and wisdom."

Included with each Weekly Knowledge is a News Flash that documents the journey that Sri Sri takes around the world and through peoples' hearts and lives. In the News Flash, Sri Sri is called Guruji, the name many have chosen to call him out of respect and love.

The journey for this collection begins on August 4, 1999 at the European Ashram in Germany and ends at the Guru Purnima Course on July 19, 2000 at Lake Tahoe, California, United States.

Table of Contents

HOW TO CONQUER JEALOUSY OR ENVY

*T*here are many ways to conquer jealousy or envy.

1. Know that the person of whom you are jealous or envious has done some good karma in the past and is now reaping the fruit.

2. See it as an inspiration to gain merit yourself.

3. Create a sense of belongingness with them. See that they are a part of you.

4. Think of all you have that they do not have and feel grateful.

5. Observe the sensations.

6. Join hands and form a team with them.

7. Realize that in the current of moving time all will perish.

8. Think of everyone who is jealous of you for what

you have and see that what they envy has not brought you joy.

9. Go and ask them, "Are you happy?"

Caroline: And what if they say, "Yes"?

If the answer is "yes" then they must be in the Art of Living! *(laughter)*

Ananda: What should you do if others are jealous or envious of you?

1. Praise them in superlatives.

2. Create a sense of belongingness in them by your kind actions.

3. Know that their feelings are temporary.

4. The best is not to recognize their envy or jealousy at all. If you recognize a feeling as a reality, it only makes your ignorance grow.

5. Know that all feelings and emotions are just passing clouds.

6. Do not show off your talents to them.

7. Know that they are puppets. They will all perish like apples and tomatoes – just with a longer shelf life. *(laughter)*

If nothing else works, just go to sleep. (*Shirley*: And don't forget to take a pillow).

News Flash
Question: With all the talk of the eclipse on the 11th of August, what should we do?

Answer: The time during an eclipse is an auspicious time for doing spiritual practices. Make sure your stomach is fairly empty. You should stop eating at least a couple of hours before the beginning of an eclipse and you may do your spiritual practices such as meditation, Kriya and satsang.

It is advisable that pregnant women and nursing mothers (for the first three months) stay indoors during the three to four hours of an eclipse.

The Art of Living and the Human Values 5H Program brochures were so nice that the Government of India borrowed the content word-for-word and made it into their own . . . but we are not jealous about it!

As usual, Bad Antogast is filled with celebration.

Jai Guru Dev

ANU VRAT

The mind lives on "more." Misery starts with "more and more." Misery makes you dense and gross.

Self is subtle. To go from gross to subtle you go through the finest relative - the atom. To overcome aversion, hatred, jealousy, attraction or entanglements, you have to go to the atom. Going to the atom means accepting a teeny tiny bit of all this.

It may be difficult to accept something that you do not like but you can definitely accept a teeny tiny bit of it - an atom. The moment you accept that one atom, you will see change happen. This has to be done in a meditative state.

Suppose you love someone. You want more and more of them, yet there is no fulfillment. In Anu Vrat - the vow of an atom - you take just one atom of that person and that is enough to bring fulfillment to you.

Though the river is vast, a little sip quenches your thirst. Though Earth has so much food, just a little bite satisfies your hunger. All that you need are tiny bits. Accept a tiny bit of everything in life - that will

4

bring you fulfillment.

Stephano: What about trouble?

There is so much trouble in the world, you can accept just a tiny part of it.

Tonight go to bed feeling that you are satisfied, taking a tiny part of divinity with you. Satisfaction comes from the subtle and not from "more and more."

Question: What about giving?

You take a tiny part, and the rest you give away.

News Flash
For a teeny tiny two minutes there was midnight at noon at Bad Antogast during the solar eclipse.

Celebration is in full swing with people from 22 countries at the European Ashram in Bad Antogast.

ART Excel teachers became teenagers and felt a big transformation in their Teacher Training Course.

The Delhi chapter of the Art of Living inaugurated the "Clean India" seva project in Delhi.

Jai Guru Dev

KNOWLEDGE AS A BURDEN

*K*nowledge is a burden if it robs you of
innocence.
Knowledge is a burden if it is not integrated into
life.
Knowledge is a burden if it does not bring joy.
Knowledge is a burden if it gives you an idea that
you are wise.
Knowledge is a burden if it does not set you free.
Knowledge is a burden if it makes you feel you are
special.

News Flash
We are accustomed to all kinds of systems - financial
systems, operational systems, management systems,
social systems. But we are oblivious to the cosmic system
that has always been present.

Transition from our little systems of functioning to the
cosmic system of functioning is what we call chaos. The
little mind blasts into the cosmic system around Guruji,
giving out laughter, pain, tears, gratitude and other

emotions. All our ashrams run on the cosmic system, and the devotees' homes are also switching to this mode of functioning.

Guruji's return to India saw a frenzy of joyous celebration with a crowd of 3,000 at the Mumbai satsang - amazing for a weekday afternoon, with virtually no publicity. From masti (ecstasy) in Mumbai, it is now bliss in Bangalore!

Jai Guru Dev

PROTECTION AND
TRANSFORMATION

*O*nly that which is temporary, small or perishable needs protection, while that which is permanent, big or vast does not.

Your body needs protection; your soul does not.
Your mind needs protection; the Self does not.

Protection simply means prolonging the time in that state; hence, protection also prevents transformation. Transformation cannot happen in protection. At the same time, without protection the desired transformation cannot happen. A seed needs protection to transform into a plant; a plant needs protection to become a tree. Protection can aid or hamper transformation. The protector should have an idea to what extent he should protect.

Kashi: Grace brings transformation with protection.

Truth does not need any protection. Both protection and transformation fall within the purview of time and space and these laws have to be honored in order to transcend time.

We are both protected and transformed. This is Hari and Hara: Hari, the protector and Hara, the transformer.

Protection is limited to time, to perishable things. How long can a doctor heal or protect someone? Forever? No. Peace and happiness do not need protection because they are not temporary.

News Flash
Onam was celebrated in the ashram with full Kerala pomp and splendor. The moon blushed and went into hiding after seeing the Divine in all His glory.

The 5H Youth Training Program is in full swing, and 5H volunteers are going into village after village.

A renowned saint of Ratnagiri Temple - who is always dressed in only a loin cloth, observes strict silence, and never moves anywhere - was eagerly awaiting Guruji's visit as ancient scriptures written 5,000 years ago had predicted his visit there.

Today Guruji begins a series of discourses on the Bhagavad Gita.

Jai Guru Dev

WHO WINS?

*M*any people quit doing seva as they put their self-image, prestige, respect, comfort and convenience ahead of their goal.

People shy away from seva when they do not receive a good position, when they get insulted, when they feel they are not getting what they expected out of it and when they consider working towards their goal a struggle rather than a challenge.

And that is why only a few people in the world succeed in reaching their goal.

What is more important to you?

News Flash
Eighty-two enthusiastic new teachers have taken off this week to spread the knowledge!

Jai Guru Dev

TWO ANECDOTES

*O*nce somebody made a mistake and Sri Sri asked him, "What punishment can I give you?"

The person replied, "Don't punish me, Guruji, I won't make the mistake again."

After some time, Sri Sri asked another person who had made a mistake, "And what punishment can I give you?"

With a bright smile Nityanand replied, "Any punishment, Guruji."

At this Sri Sri turned to the rest of us with a smile and said, "See, he is so confident of my love for him that he is not afraid of any punishment."

Where there is love, there is no fear.
Do not be afraid of being punished by God.
Trust in the love that He has for you.

It was Arun and Chitra's wedding anniversary. They presented an ornate fan to Sri Sri, saying, "A fan from two grateful fans."

At this Sri Sri said, "Devotees are the fan; God is the air. The air is always there, but the fans make you feel it. God is always there; devotees make His presence felt!"

News Flash
And three more miracles . . .
On a domestic flight in the U.S., Manjesh's mother fainted. A checkup later showed that her aorta had dilated and the doctors suggested an immediate operation. She visited Guruji in San Jose, and when she went for a checkup again, her aorta was back to its normal size! The doctors could not believe this miracle.

Mr. Sardana from Delhi could not even walk - he was advised to have a heart transplant and total bed rest. He somehow made it to both the Basic and Advanced Courses, and his doctors were amazed to find his heart absolutely normal! Now he walks happily all over the ashram.

In Deesa, Gujarat, a boy who was deaf-mute since birth, started speaking and hearing after his first Sudarshan Kriya!

Many such experiences are being reported from all over. Lord Krishna's birthday was celebrated in all gaiety at the ashram. Devotees danced and played - transported back 5,000 years!

Bangalore saw its biggest ever satsang this week.

Jai Guru Dev

Compassion And Karma

*T*here are two types of compassion. One is the compassion of the wise, one is that of the ignorant.

An ignorant person's compassion is toward the fruit of an action – the sickness or suffering that he witnesses. But a wise person's compassion is toward the lack of knowledge – the underlying reason for sickness or suffering.

Compassion for suffering shows ignorance. Suffering comes because of karma, and if you believe in karma, where is compassion? One reaps the fruit of one's actions.

If a judge has compassion for all the offenders, then the jails will be empty. At the same time, are the judges cruel to the offenders? No. The judges' compassion is for the lack of knowledge, not for the suffering of the criminals. It is the criminals' karma.

Often people think compassion is an act, an action. Know that compassion is your very nature. Then you will see that karma and compassion are not contradictory but complement each other.

Suppose two people come to a hospital. One is suffering from starvation, the other is ill from overeating. What type of compassion should the doctor have toward each of them? This is a riddle for you to solve!

News Flash
The Youth Training Program ended this week on a jubilant note as 230 Yuvacharyas set forth on their mission to transform rural India. In less than three weeks, these youngsters acquired skills in disciplines as varied as martial arts, organic farming and directing plays. They presented a splendid cultural program on the concluding day. This course showed once again that grace and knowledge have the power to transform raw material into polished gems!

The festival of Lord Ganesha is being celebrated with gusto all over India. In two districts in Karnataka, senior government officers have advised all schools to conduct ART Excel courses.

Jai Guru Dev

NEGATIVITY NEEDS AN ANCHOR

*N*egativity cannot remain without a support.

Positivity, happiness can exist without any reason.

The mind goes on trying to find support for its
negativity. It looks for a hook on which to hang its
negativity - if not this person, then that thing or that
person. This perpetuates maya!

The creeping vine of negativity needs a support in
order to grow. But negativity or aversion for even one
person can guarantee a one-way ticket to hell - you
need nothing else!

All negativity is an indicator for you to move to the
center and to broaden your vision to cosmic
intelligence. Instead of focusing your attention on
support for your negativity, look at the seed of
negativity.

With meditation, silence and Kriya, the source of
negativity is nipped at the root.

16

News Flash
Bangalore saw its biggest and best ever satsang - nearly
2,000 people were outside the jam-packed hall, but were
smilingly watching the proceedings on a large screen!

A new seva project was inaugurated by Guruji in
Urugahalli, a village adopted by the Art of Living. The
project helped over 200 young women become self-
employed.

Several other villages have benefited from our seva
projects as we provided water supplies, electricity and
buildings under the 5H Program.

The ashram is bursting with joy with more than 800
blissful faces!

Jai Guru Dev

LIFE IS A WAR

*L*ife is a war.

Doctors fight against disease.
Lawyers fight against injustice.
Teachers fight against ignorance.

Depression happens when you lose the will to fight.
Arjuna was depressed; he did not want to fight. His
bow fell from his hands and his fingers trembled.
Krishna urged him to wake up and fight! The decision
to fight can take away your depression as it did for
Arjuna.

Bharat: Fight until you give up.

Prashant: Not give up . . . give in! (*laughter*)

Even your body is a battlefield.

News Flash
There were two glorious Advanced Courses and a fantastic Teacher Training Course. The ashram was lit up with more than 2,000 happy faces. Two Shankaracharyas met Guruji. Swami Swatantranandji regaled us with stories from the Puranas. The ashram is getting ready for the Navratri celebrations that will start early next week.

Jai Guru Dev

SPIRITUALITY AND CELEBRATION

*C*elebration is the nature of the spirit.
Any celebration has to be spiritual.
A celebration without spirituality has no depth.
Silence gives depth to celebration.

Some people think being silent is spirituality. For example, many meditators feel that laughing, singing and dancing are not spiritual.

Some people think only celebration is spirituality. For example, in some parts of the world, such as rural India or Africa, celebration means loud music; there is no silence at all.

Spirituality is a harmonious blend of outer silence and inner celebration; and also inner silence and outer celebration!

News Flash
His Holiness the Dalai Lama was in Bangalore and met Guruji. He was all praise for the help Art of Living

programs have provided to India and the world. He lauded Guruji for his success in reviving the ancient Indian Vedic heritage and presenting it to the world in such an accessible way in a modern context.

At the recent International Youth Meeting on Human Values organized by the United Nations in Seoul, South Korea, the Art of Living Foundation played a stellar role. Out of the nearly 1,000 non-governmental organizations participating, the Art of Living was the only workshop mentioned in the plenary session.

Navratri celebrations at the ashram were a combination of bubbling joy, deep meditation and profound silence. Among the many saints who graced the occasion were the Shankaracharya and Swami Swatantranand with his humor-filled discourses on the Bhagvatam. Thanks to the excellent video arrangements, the thousands who came were able to participate fully in all the celebrations. Next year we plan to go live on the Internet.

Jai Guru Dev

SOUND FAITH

*H*ave faith in sound and move on to have faith in silence. Have faith in sound when it is pleasant and have faith in silence when sound is unpleasant.

When someone says something bad, you immediately believe it and the mind becomes more disturbed. Believing in an unpleasant sound creates more turmoil in the mind. In that situation shift your faith to silence.

Have faith in sound, like the chanting of mantras.

People seem to have more faith in chatting and gossip rather than chanting and knowledge. Have faith in knowledge and chanting, and have faith in silence.

Anecdote
On the day of the full moon, Sri Sri visited the ancient temple of Kollur where there was an elaborately decorated chariot of the goddess being pulled around the temple. Explaining its significance,

Sri Sri said that each one of us is like a chariot carrying the power of God within. We are the real chariot of the Divine. Our body is the chariot and the soul is the deity that is being pulled around to purify the world.

News Flash
Steady rains could not stop over 8,000 people in Mangalore and over 1,000 people in Mysore from singing, dancing and soaking in Guruji's presence.

Jai Guru Dev

ALWAYS?

*H*ow can you always be happy? Forget about "always," then you will be happy.

In always wanting to be comfortable, one becomes lazy.
In always wanting perfection, one becomes angry.
In always wanting to be rich, one becomes greedy.

Fear comes when we do not realize that only life is for always.

This projection of the nature of self - which is "always" - onto the temporal - which can never be "always" - is called maya.

All ways do not lead you, only one way leads you.

If you remove "always" from your dictionary, then everything is "all right." Drop "always" and all will be right - that is intelligence.

News Flash
Guruji was the chief guest at a Muslim gathering where he spoke on "Human Values and the Prophet Mohammed."

Guruji initiated a revolutionary movement among 24 prominent saints of India to welcome His Holiness Pope John Paul II to India, an event that was publicized in several national newspapers.

In the week that passed, Guruji said that it was a "free" week with not many appointments but he ended up being busier than when he was supposed to be "busy."

Jai Guru Dev

BEING IN UTTER LOVE

An example inspires and brings confidence in the application of knowledge, and the visible sign of it is an undying smile.

The Self knows neither sorrow nor death, yet in it flow all the relative events.

It is easy to be detached when you are not in love. Being in utter love, and yet undisturbed, caring yet not worried, persistent yet not perturbed, are all the obvious signs of the Self shining through!

News Flash
Diwali celebrations saw unbounded joy and Guruji gave full expression to it with a spellbinding dance! One renowned Swamiji commented, "I have narrated the Bhagvatam for decades, but now I have experienced Dwapar (the age of Krishna) for the first time."

This tidal wave continued from the banks of the Ganges at Rishikesh to Varanasi, where more than 4,000 swayed in bliss.

There is a saying - "Kashi Dhama Marnat Mukti" - dying in Kashi (also known as Varanasi), you attain salvation. Guruji won over everybody's hearts by commenting that now, even while **living** in Kashi, people could attain salvation.

The Touring Tornado held a hurricane satsang at Delhi and then moved on to Hardwar for the immersion of Amma's ashes.

Jai Guru Dev

HOMAGE TO AMMA

*G*uruji's mother, our beloved Amma, left her physical body in a peaceful and meditative state at 1 p.m. on November 9, 1999 in Bangalore, just as Guruji set foot in the holy city of Varanasi, precisely as he had predicted a few days earlier. For those present around Guruji, it was an amazing experience to feel the depth of love and not an iota of grief. It was a celebration of knowledge never before experienced. Even as the news came, Guruji kept meeting people and addressed the big satsang with the same smile as always.

All her life Amma served with love, humor and dynamism, extending her motherly love to one and all. She had an unparalleled love for Guruji and shared a unique relationship with him - he was not only a son, but also a mentor. Hundreds of people bid a moving farewell to Amma, singing Jai Jai Radha Raman.

Amma's mortal ashes were brought to Delhi and Guruji accompanied them to Hardwar and immersed them in the holy Ganges there. Some of her ashes were also immersed in the river Cauvery, on whose banks Amma grew up.

On November 9, Guruji was the chief guest at the consecration of the Vishalakshi temple at Varanasi, an invitation that had come two months earlier. At this very temple, Guruji's grandfather had prayed 73 years ago and was blessed with Amma. Creation returned to its source as Guruji reinstalled the very same ancient deity from whom Amma got her name, on the very same day that she left for her heavenly abode.

The Art of Living family is greatly indebted to Amma and seeks her blessings. The memorial service was held on November 21 and all chapters were requested to have satsangs that day. Through this event the Art of Living has shown to the world that not only life, but death, can be a celebration.

Jai Guru Dev

Death And Spirituality

*D*eath brings you in touch with the reality of life.
Death creates a vacuum, a void.
Void is fertile ground for the spirit to manifest.
All talents, inventions and creativity spring
forth from the void.
Creation has a tendency to return to the void.

Bharat: All problems come when you avoid the void.
(*laughter*)

All the places of worship in all religions are connected
with places of burial or cremation because the
awareness of death alone can bring dispassion and
make you well grounded in knowledge.

According to Indian mythology, the abode of Siva is
in Mount Kailasa, as well as in Smashana - the
cremation ground. Kailasa means "where there is only
celebration" and Smashana is "where there is only
void."

Thus Divinity dwells in the void as well as in
celebration. In you there is void; in you there is
celebration.

News Flash
ART Excel children avoided sweets, colas and fireworks this Diwali festival and saved the money to sponsor children in the tribal school.

In the Rishikesh Advanced Course hall there is no void, only celebration! Profound knowledge and immense love radiate from Guruji.

In a devotee's house in Bhubaneshwar, Orissa, Guruji's photograph turned red just before the cyclone and returned to normal after the cyclone was over. Some devotees from Orissa actually made it to Rishikesh despite the catastrophic conditions in the state. One lady shared that she was in a meeting with about 50 people, when she felt that Guruji was sending her a message. Closing her eyes, she prayed to Guruji and then immediately advised everyone to evacuate the city. Later it was discovered that the entire area, including that building, was submerged in the deluge. She thanked Guruji with tears of gratitude for saving their lives.

Our volunteers are already engaged in seva and relief work in Orissa.

Jai Guru Dev

AGGRESSION AS A WAY TO OVERCOME DEPRESSION

*L*ack of idealism is the main cause of depression among youth today. Life appears to be so meaningless to these children, who are either too scared of the competitive world or too bogged down by heavy stimuli. They need an inspiration, and spirituality is the inspiration that can keep the spirit up!

Aggression is the antidote to depression.
Depression sets in if there is a lack of zeal to fight.
Depression is the lack of energy; anger and aggression are a bolt of energy.

When Arjuna was depressed, Krishna inspired him to fight and thus reinstated life back into Arjuna.

If you are depressed, do not take Prozac - just fight for any cause.

If aggression crosses a certain limit, it leads you back into depression. That is what happened with King Ashoka who won the Kalinga war but became depressed. He had to take refuge in Buddha.

Wise are those who do not fall either into aggression or depression. That is the golden rule of a Yogi.

Just wake up and acknowledge you are a Yogi.

News Flash
The two Advanced Courses in Rishikesh were simply out of this world. Guruji flew to Bangalore for a day for the memorial service of his most beloved Amma. People had come from all parts of India to pay homage to the great lady who gave Guruji to this world. Guruji did Aarti to Amma's portrait, singing the same song that Amma used to sing when she did Aarti to him. Tears flowed from everyone. Guruji shared a few anecdotes about Amma. It was no coincidence that Amma left the body on Yama Dwitiya and that Vaikuntha Samaradhana fell on Vaikuntha Chaturdashi Day (the day when Godliness wakes up.)

He then flew back to Delhi where he addressed thousands in a mind-boggling satsang, then on to Indore where huge cutouts and welcome arches greeted Guruji. The indoor stadium was packed to its capacity of 20,000. The following day saw over 40,000 people spellbound in meditation at the open-air stadium. This was telecast live on local TV. Guruji has devised a new way of giving darshan – all 40,000 were satisfied. Guess how!

Jai Guru Dev

THINK FRESH

To think fresh you need to be free of all impressions. Let go of all impressions right this moment and be hollow and empty. When you hear a word, the sound conveys the meaning instantaneously. Similarly, the knowledge that you are sitting, standing or talking needs neither confirmation nor proof.

Just an intention to be free makes you free right away. Realization that freedom is your very nature brings enormous Shakti (energy).

Forget about this knowledge sheet and be fresh! (*laughter*)

News Flash
Mumbai media provided excellent coverage of Guruji's visit there. The football stadium at Cooperage held over 50,000 people spellbound in meditation and satsang. Everyone was welcomed with sandalwood paste and sweets. Guruji visited blind women in a shelter named after him.

Then on to Cochin in Kerala, where an interfaith convention was attended by thousands. The Imam of Trivandrum and the Bishop of Cochin praised the Art of Living Foundation's work in elevating human values. Several senior government officials and dignitaries took part in the program.

A traffic policeman in Cochin suddenly got a glimpse of Guruji and started giving wrong signals ("with a blissful smile on his face," Raghu adds). In the evening, Guruji served dinner for all the volunteers before leaving Kottayam. Even though there was a political strike throughout Kerala, only Art of Living vehicles plied smoothly on the roads and only Art of Living satsangs were held as scheduled.

Jai Guru Dev

THE FIVE SECRETS

*T*here are five secrets that are sacred and are guarded by the subtle beings and angels in this creation. They are:

Jananarahasya (the secret of birth) - Birth is a secret. How a soul takes a body, the criteria for selecting the place of birth, time of birth, type of body and parents are all a secret.

Maranarahasya (the secret of death) - Death is a highly guarded secret. Death remains a mystery. The process of separation of spirit from matter and its journey from then on is a secret.

Rajarahasya (the royal secret, the secret of ruling) - The principles of governing, the principles of maintaining orderliness in creation are a secret.

Prakritirahasya (the secret of nature) - Nature is a mystery. The more you know about nature, the more the mystery deepens. The more a scientist knows, the more he feels there is much more to know. Science, though appearing to resolve the mystery in creation, has deepened it. The knowledge of particles, wave functions, black holes, the vacuum state have only deepened the mystery.

Mantrarahasya (the secret of mantras) - The mantras and their effect, influence, method and mode of working are all a mystery. Mantras are the impulses or rhythms of consciousness, which itself is a mystery.

Usually in the West, a secret is shameful and dishonest. But in the East, it is honored and regarded as sacred.

News Flash
Guruji's tour of seven cities in Kerala saw thousands of people coming to satsangs, culminating in the grandest ever satsang and meditation of the millennium. Over 75,000 people sat enraptured in meditation for half an hour in pin-drop silence in Thiruvananthapuram, the capital city of Kerala.

Our teachers Nitin Limaye and Bharat Shirur, representing Guruji and the Art of Living Foundation, addressed the World Parliament of Religions in Cape Town, South Africa this week.

Want to see wild elephants? You do not need to visit Africa. These days 40 to 50 wild elephants have been visiting the ashram school and lakes by night.

Jai Guru Dev

THE WISDOM OF SECRETS

A wise person makes no effort to conceal a secret. But he does not make an effort to reveal a secret either. For example, you do not talk about menstruation or death to a five-year-old, but as they grow older these things are not hidden from them anymore. They become known as a matter of course.

An unenlightened one tries to protect a secret; and he also reveals the secret at the wrong time, to the wrong person, in the wrong place, and makes a big fuss about secrets.

Trying to protect a secret causes anxiety and discomfort.

An ignorant one is not comfortable with a secret, whether revealed or unrevealed, but the wise one is comfortable with a secret, whether revealed or unrevealed.

News Flash
Prominent leaders of the Jain community are meeting in the Bangalore Ashram to discuss Ahimsa - nonviolence - on the 2,600th anniversary of Lord Mahavira.

Jai Guru Dev

WISDOM FOR ORGANIZERS

*K*nowledge has organizing power. Only knowledge can organize. The more steeped you are in knowledge, the better you can organize.

Never underestimate your organization. If you underestimate your organization, you will not be able to build it.

Defend your intentions, not your actions. Often people defend their actions and lose sight of their intentions. Then they feel sorry and weak. There is no need to feel sorry. Defend your intention to do right.

Teamwork. In teamwork, you achieve more than you do individually. Certain work is best done alone and other work is best done with a team. Find the balance between walking alone and working with a team. In either case, alone or with a team, you will face obstacles. For your growth, both are essential. Each has its disadvantages and advantages. Drop any one, and you will be at a loss. The skill is not to have an aversion to either and to focus on the goal.

Defending friends. Suppose you have introduced a friend to a job and they make a mistake. Do not try to defend them. That is where the team breaks up. When you defend a friend, you are not friendly to everybody. Defending someone's mistakes does not do justice to the teamwork and stops the person from learning. Soft-heartedness and compassion in an organization can be detrimental to both the teamwork and the organization.

Never justify a mistake with intimidation or logic. Raising your voice, intimidation, anger, shouting and applying erroneous logic makes a wrong appear right. Do not give in to that. Do not give into assertiveness, intimidation, wrong logic and soft-heartedness.

Working with volunteers. Volunteers often act as though everyone's a boss and not a worker. When working with volunteers, be calm and quiet. Ask, "Have you finished your work?"

Solutions will always be ad hoc. The more dynamic an institution is, the more the solutions will be ad hoc. Its not like a nine-to-five company job where roles are designed and planned for a year. With volunteers, the productivity is more intense. The more dynamic a group, the quicker things happen. Maintaining a margin for confusion and chaos can prevent stress.

Jai Guru Dev

INTENTION

*I*ntentions keep the tension in. Being hollow and empty means dropping all intentions. Within tension, rest does not become deep. But devotion dissolves intentions.

Intention pushes you to the future yet bliss is always in the present. The one who wakes up to this truth is wise. Occasionally, if an intention arises in a state of bliss, the intention manifests effortlessly.

The more intentions you have, the more "in tension" you will be. To minimize your intentions could be your last intention.

News Flash
Guruji's stay in India concluded with a grand celebration with more than 7,000 people from all over Bangalore. The Bangalore devotees published a bhajan cassette and a beautiful pictorial book in memory of Amma. The Art of Living was invited by leaders of the Jain community to join them in celebrating the 2,600th anniversary of

Mahavira's birth. We were also invited to participate in the millennium celebration with the Dalai Lama at Varanasi.

The brightest moon of the millennium lit up the snow and the smiling faces that welcomed Guruji to his home in Europe.

Jai Guru Dev

THE NATURE OF THE FIVE SENSES
IS KNOWLEDGE

*E*very cell in your body has the ability of all five senses. You can see without the eyes. Vision is part of consciousness. That is why in dreams you can see without the eyes. You can feel without the skin. That is why people without limbs can still feel sensations in their missing limbs. You can smell without the nose and taste without the tongue.

When someone says something, you are all ears - you are listening with every cell of your body. There is the expression "looking with a thousand eyes" - one is all eyes.

The five senses and the ability to think are all present in consciousness. So each cell of the body has the potential to perform all the functions of the senses.

All cells are made of the same tissue - each DNA molecule contains all functions of the body. Consciousness is inherent in all the cells.

Every sensory stimulus brings knowledge, which is the nature of consciousness. Sight brings some knowledge

- blue, red, green. Knowing is the nature of consciousness.

Vikas: Some people who have lost one of their senses find that the others become heightened.

Sri Sri: You do not have to lose one to sharpen the others. You can sharpen all of them in deep silence.

Mikey: What happens when you have no sense?

Sri Sri: You become like Mikey! (*room explodes with laughter*)

New Year's Exercise
Feel that every cell has the potential to see and hear - all eyes and ears. Sit comfortably, easily. Close the eyes. Know that you are all eyes, all ears.

News Flash
*Two new books, the fourth volume of **An Intimate Note to the Sincere Seeker** and **Wisdom for the New Millennium**, have been released.*

A huge Christmas tree adorned the meditation hall in Bad Antogast for the glorious Christmas celebration with gifts of wisdom and grace; everyone was gift wrapped in smiles and knowledge.

The Massachusetts Institute of Technology (MIT) in Boston has introduced the Art of Living program as part of its curriculum.

Thirteen hundred people have assembled on the Mediterranean in an indoor stadium with the master to celebrate and welcome the new millennium.

Jai Guru Dev

FIVE FACTORS THAT INFLUENCE THE MIND

*T*here are five factors that influence the mind: place, time, food, past impressions, and associations and actions.

Every place you are in has a different impact on the mind. Even in your house you can see that you feel differently in different rooms. A place where there has been singing, chanting and meditation has a different influence on the mind. Suppose you like a particular place; you may find that a little later it will not be the same.

Time is also a factor. Different times of the day and year have different influences on the mind.

Different types of food that you eat influence you for several days.

Past impressions - karmas - have a different impact on the mind. Awareness, alertness, knowledge and meditation all help erase past impressions.

Associations and actions, or the people and events you are associated with, also influence your mind. In certain company your mind behaves in one way and with others your mind behaves in a different way.

Question: Should we worry about them?

Sri Sri: No need to be paranoid about it. Just know these factors.

Though these five factors influence life and the mind, know that the Self is much more powerful. As you grow in knowledge, you will influence them all.

News Flash
About 1,300 people from over 41 countries gathered to celebrate the New Millennium Satsang and Advanced Course at Massa di Carrara, Tuscany, Italy. As the sun set, everyone gathered on the shore of the Mediterranean with Guruji, chanting Om to say goodbye to the passing millennium. They were uplifted and inspired by a silent meditation at midnight and satsang with bhajans in many languages. The Advanced Course participants were so blissed out that the French translator spoke into the Italian earphones for 40 minutes and the French had no translation, yet no one commented.

Satsangs and New Years Advanced Courses were held around the world in over 93 countries to welcome the new millennium.

On January 6, Guruji spoke on Italian national television as part of the continuing celebration.

Dog Story: There was this man who walked his dog every day for seven years. On this particular day he goes to walk the dog and the dog misbehaves and runs away from him, and runs for about ten minutes. The dog had never done this before! The man finds him standing under a pole with a poster announcing the Milano satsang. So the man sees him standing there and the dog won't move. This forces him to read the poster. He decides that the dog ran away because he wanted the man to see the poster. The man called about the satsang and said he and his friends were coming. The dog led the men and his friends to the Divine.

"Ever New Happy You!"

Jai Guru Dev

REASONS TO BE WITH A GURU

*T*here are six main reasons to be with a guru.

1. You would like to have your wishes fulfilled, and being with the guru is more pleasurable.

2. Everything else looks more painful to you and you come for comfort.

3. You want to evolve and become enlightened; you want to attain higher knowledge.

4. You have a vision or goal that you share with the guru, whom you see as a missionary or visionary.

5. You are there just to serve and to give comfort to the guru.

6. You are with the guru because you belong to the guru. There is no choice.

News Flash
The President of Italy sent a message congratulating the Art of Living Foundation for its contributions and wishing success with our program.

The Art of Living Foundation also received an unofficial message from the Vatican saying they cannot officially support our activities but they will not interfere.

It was a moving scene at the completion of the Central Jail prisoner's program in Bangalore. The State Inspector General of Police had boundless praise for the selfless service of the Art of Living teachers and volunteers.

Jai Guru Dev

EVOLUTION: NOT PART OF THE SELF

*A*re you evolving? If you are evolving, you are not in the Self. But you are not out of the Self, because nothing can exist out of the Self. (*laughter*)

There are six distortions that do not exist in the Self.

1. Expansion - Prasarana. Expansion implies there is something into which to expand. That which expands cannot be the basis for expansion.

2. Contraction - Akunchana. Contraction means something shrinks from something else. Self does not withdraw or shrink from anything, so contraction does not exist in the Self.

3. Evolution - Vriddhi. Evolution is the process of becoming something that does not already exist. Self is always the same, so it cannot evolve.

4. Decay - Kshaya. There is no devolution or decay in the Self. It does not get old or stale. That is why when you are close to your Self, you do not feel that you are aging.

5. Beginning - Anaadi. Self has no beginning. If God has a beginning, then He is not God.

6. Lack - Abhava. Self has no lack. Whatever lacks something is not complete. Self does not lack anything; it is complete. Lack indicates the existence of something outside itself that does not exist for the Self. So if you feel you have not grown at all, do not worry, you are close to the Self. (laughter)

When your mind is with the Self, then you do not worry about evolution. If you are thinking about evolving, then you are stuck in the mind. Mind is part of the matter, and matter evolves and decays.

That is how the experience of contraction and expansion is all play and display of the mind. Mind expands and contracts. When it expands, it comes close to the truth, which has no expansion.

Are you still evolving? Good luck!

News Flash
A distressed devotee went to Guruji this week when her pregnant daughter began to hemorrhage and the baby was thought by the doctors to be dead. The next

day news came that the bleeding had stopped and the baby's heartbeat was again detected.

After a weekend of intimate satsangs with the devotees in Holland, Guruji returned to Bad Antogast at the European Ashram.

Jai Guru Dev

VARIETIES OF SPIRIT

*W*hy should you think God is only one? Why cannot God also be many? If God made man in His own image, what image is He? African, Mongolian, Caucasian, Japanese, Filipino? Why are there so many types of man and so many varieties of things?

There is not just one type of tree, not just one type of snake, cloud, mosquito or vegetable. There is not just one type of anything, so why should God be only one? How could this consciousness that manifested this whole creation and that loves variety, be monotonous? God loves variety, so He must be of infinite variety Himself. God manifests in many names, forms and varieties.

Some schools of thought do not give God the freedom to appear in His many forms. They want Him in one uniform!

You change your appearance to suit the occasion. When such is the case, how could you think there is no variety in the Spirit? Ancient people knew this and that is why they cognized the Divinity as infinite qualities and forms. The Spirit is not dull and boring.

The Spirit that is the basis of creation is dynamic and ever changing. God is not only one, but many!

When you accept the variety of Divinity, you cease to be a fanatic or a fundamentalist.

Tommy: God is many, God is one, He made so many just for fun.

News Flash
Howdy ya'll! After an intimate East Texas Advanced Course, Guruji's entourage took the Alamo (San Antonio, Texas) by storm. Satsang - brimming with bliss, laughter, the flow of knowledge and love - washed over the devotees. After ten years, Guruji is back at home deep in the heart of Texas.

Jai Guru Dev

THE PROBLEM'S TAIL

Sri Sri: There is no problem that cannot be solved.

Someone: I have a few I can give you. (*laughter*)

Sri Sri: When you have a problem and you think it cannot be solved, you have accepted it. Then it is no longer a problem, it is a fact.

For example, suppose you think it is a problem that the ocean in Norway is too cold. Obviously, you cannot heat the ocean. If it cannot be solved, you accept it and it is no longer a problem. Only when you are searching for a solution is there a problem and so there is no problem that cannot be solved. The moment you realize there is no solution, a problem ceases to be a problem.

The solution is the tail of every problem. Solutions come to you when:
    You are calm and collected.
    You use intelligence.
    You are not lethargic but active.
    You have strong faith in Divine Law.

Kai: If you don't want any problems, you can have a guru.

Sheila: If you want all the problems of all the people, become a guru.

Tom: You cannot solve a problem when you focus on the problem alone. But when you step up to your real need, your real goal, to the higher Self, you find many solutions.

News Flash
Snow followed Guruji from Dallas to Oslo.

Spontaneous and contagious laughing meditations followed Guruji's public talks in Hamburg and Oslo.

Riding the waves of bliss, Guruji's giggling Gopi Gang went ice skating.

On to Copenhagen tomorrow.

Jai Guru Dev

DO NOT WORSHIP OR IDOLIZE

Worshipping or idolizing without a sense of belonging is always futile. Such worship only causes fear and distance.

There are others who are paranoid about worship. They get irritated when they see others worshipping.

The modes of worship or idolizing may be different in different parts of the world. Some worship the Pope; others worship pop stars; some are crazy about politicians. Look at all the children; they worship their heroes on posters all over the walls.

Adoration alone makes you a fan. A sense of belonging and seeing the divinity in those whom you adore makes you a saint.

Raghu: You mean we can see divinity in a pop star or a politician?

Sri Sri: If you can, it is a divinity that is distorted. (*laughter*)

Those who worship without a sense of belonging and

those who are against worship are in the same boat, as both are clogged with fear.

The Bible says, "I am your God. You shall have no other gods before me." The same is said in the ancient Indian scriptures. "One who worships God as separate from the 'I am' consciousness is dull-headed," and "Poojo aur na deva" - do not worship other gods.

The offering, the offered and the offerer are all ONE.

News Flash
In Copenhagen, a thrilled audience of 900 was enraptured with Divya's and Craig's music. The excellent teamwork of the Denmark Art of Living made a memorable satsang.

About 18,000 people did the Basic Course over a three-week period in Ahmedabad, a city in Gujarat, India. One of our youth leaders addressed a gathering of 20,000 people and inspired them about the 5H program.

After ten years of developing the Prison SMART program, one of our teachers, Tom Duffy, will be acknowledged by the Lower Cape Youth Congress with an Outstanding Achievement Award for Service to America's Youth.

Jai Guru Dev

FEEL THE PINCH

A devotee asked Sri Sri: Please forgive me if I have committed a mistake.

Sri Sri: Why should you be forgiven? You are asking for forgiveness because you feel a pinch and you want to be free from it, is this not true? Let the pinch be there. The pinch will not let the mistake happen again. Forgiveness removes the pinch and you keep repeating the mistake!

Question: How do you know a mistake is a mistake?

Sri Sri: A mistake is something that gives you a pinch. If it has not pinched you, it is not a mistake at all. It is the pinch that irks the consciousness and that pinch disallows the mistake to be repeated. Be with the pinch and not the guilt. It is a very fine balance.

Question: What is the difference between guilt and a pinch?

Sri Sri: Guilt is about a specific action and a pinch is about a specific result or happening. You can only feel guilty about what you did - not about what happened.

But whatever happened, whether because of you or someone else, it can cause a pinch in you.

Question: How do we get over the guilt?

Tom: Just blame the boss! (*laughter*)

Sri Sri: You can get over the guilt through wisdom, by knowing the nature of mind, the nature of consciousness and by having a broader perspective of the phenomenon.

Question: Can we learn from our mistakes without feeling the pinch?

Sri Sri: Learning is at an intellectual level while you feel the pinch at an emotional level. The drive of your emotions is much stronger than your intellect, so a pinch will not let the mistake recur.

Bharat: We feel guilt where we have control, at the intellectual level. But a pinch is at the emotional level where we do not have control.

Question: So, should we discard the intellect?

Sri Sri: You cannot be driven by your emotions alone. Your intellect acts as a brake for your emotions.

Feel the pinch. The pinch will create an awareness that what happened was beyond your capacity. The awareness will bring you to surrender. Surrender will free you from guilt.

So, the steps of evolution are from pinch to awareness to surrender to freedom.

News Flash
Chinese New Year - the Year of the Dragon - was celebrated in the ashram. The International Advanced Course began in jet lag and ended in bliss!

Jai Guru Dev

SKILL IN PRAISING

*O*ften when you praise, you praise in comparison to someone else. In order to praise one person, we put down someone else and when we want to point out somebody's mistake, we praise another.

Some are stingy in praising, and some are shy.
Some are simply not accustomed to praising.
Some praise with motives, and some praise just to elevate.
Others praise themselves in order to hide their low self-esteem.
But real praise dawns in a blossomed state of consciousness.

The praise that comes out of an elevated state of consciousness is simply its nature and is quite different. Normally praise comes out of craving and pride. Praise that comes from a heightened consciousness always comes out of fulfillment.

Praising can no doubt elevate the consciousness and bring enthusiasm and energy. At the same time it can also bring arrogance. Praising is a skill.

When someone praises you, do you take it without shying away? Accepting praise without shyness is also a skill.

News Flash
The hot weather at the Bangalore Ashram was dispelled by cool showers of grace. Agastya Nadi - a system of prediction through 5,000-year-old inscriptions on palm leaves - was brought to the ashram and amazed people by very accurate readings of their past.

Adi Chunchungiri Swamiji, one of the renowned pontiffs of South India, visited the ashram.

Sixty enthusiastic people bid a loud farewell to 100 very lucky people "flying" by train with Guruji to Belgaum near Goa.

Jai Guru Dev

NEWS FLOOD

*T*his week we had so much news that we are sending just a news flood.

It has been an unusually hectic week even by Guruji's standards. Last Friday, Guruji addressed three satsangs in a single day, starting with a rural satsang among thousands of poor people of Inchilla, a brief stopover with the enthusiastic devotees of Belgaum, and on to the urban elite of Goa, with the sound of our bhajans reverberating everywhere.

Ahmedabad was all keyed up as Guruji returned after a two-year gap - teachers from all over Gujarat had been working together to make this the biggest satsang ever. In the morning, over 25,000 people did the Sudarshan Kriya conducted live by Guruji. A cosmic rhythm was set in motion. Intense experiences, strong fragrances, and changes in the weather pattern occurred as three eagles circled directly overhead, joined by a flock of other birds. Many people stated that their entire life until now was on one side and this event on the other - such was the magnitude of the experience for them. Kriya was followed by an elaborate lunch for the participants - the network of volunteers had organized 60 counters to feed everyone.

In the evening the same cricket stadium was transformed, with a huge lotus constructed in the stands for Guruji to sit in, and video screens all over the grounds. Streams of people flooded in, excited and happy even before the program began. The crowd totaled nearly 200,000. The traffic diversion for the event was announced by the traffic police well in advance, and the event took place without any chaos.

Following 27 minutes of total, still meditation, the entire crowd was on its feet, singing and dancing. The subinspector of police remarked that even though a meager force of 500 was deployed, they had nothing to do, so blissful and orderly was the crowd. The policemen hugged people and confessed that only their uniforms prevented them from joining the dance. The high priests of the ancient city of Dwarka (Krishna's capital) came all the way to invite Guruji and placed a resplendent turban from the temple deity on his head.

The next day was the foundation-laying ceremony of the Gujarat Ashram on the banks of the river Mahi. After a brief satsang in Vidyanagar, Guruji addressed over 3,000 ART Excel youth - it was the best ever question-and-answer session, with witty one-line exchanges between the little ones and the wise one.

Enthusiastic devotees with a live band awaited Guruji at 4 a.m. in Jamnagar. Guruji visited the ancient capital of Krishna in Dwarka for a Vishnu Yagna in the ancient Dwarkadheesh Temple. The entire city danced as Guruji was taken in a horse-drawn carriage through the streets of Dwarka - it was a nonstop celebration.

That evening, we had another divine satsang in Jamnagar, before returning to Ahmedabad. The blissful ones are now in Delhi, en route to Rishikesh.

Postscript: The three-year-old daughter of one of our devotees fell from a three-story building recently. Later she said to her parents, "That bearded uncle whose photo we have at home - he caught me!" She escaped totally unhurt. (Caution: Please do not try this at home!)

Jai Guru Dev

FORM AND FORMLESS, AGGRESSION AND INTUITION

Form and Formless

Life is a combination of form and formless. Feelings have no form but their expressions have form. The Self has no form but its abode has form.

Similarly, wisdom and grace have no form but are expressed through form.

Discarding the formless, you become inert, materialistic and paranoid.

Discarding the form, you become a lost ascetic, a space cadet or an emotional wreck!

Aggression and Intuition

Aggression and assertiveness overshadow intuition.

Often, people who are sensitive tend to become aggressive in order to avoid being hurt.

In this process, they lose sight of their fine intuition.

Fine intuition needs sensitivity, but sensitivity is often painful.

In order to avoid pain one becomes aggressive and assertive, and in turn loses one's intuitive ability.

Intuition is close to the truth.

Often, aggression and assertiveness thrive on the idea of truthfulness - an aggressive person is convinced of the rightness of his position.

To be truthful, you do not need to be aggressive and assertive.

News Flash
At the World Presidents' Organization (WPO), Guruji delivered the keynote address which was lauded by a standing ovation.

Over 3,000 people participated in the Shivratri celebrations at Rishikesh, where the all-night satsang and darshan line culminated in a live Kriya at dawn.

Following Guruji's visit, 28 Basic Courses with nearly 8,500 participants started this week in Ahmedabad.

Around 60 Art of Living teachers are in Rishikesh, planning strategies to develop various areas. Prison programs and 5H programs are in full swing all over India.

Jai Guru Dev

THE GOAL OF ALL ANSWERS

*S*ome questions can only be answered in silence. Silence is the goal of all answers. If an answer does not silence the mind, it is no answer.

Thoughts are not the goal in themselves. Their goal is silence. When you ask the question "Who am I?" you get no answer, there is only silence. That is the real answer. Your soul is solidified silence and this solidified silence is wisdom, knowledge.

The easy way to silence the thoughts is to arouse the feelings, for only through feelings will peace, joy and love dawn. They are all your very nature.

To the question "Who am I?" the only relevant answer is silence. You need to discard all answers in words, including "I am nothing" or "I am the cosmic self" or "I am the Self." Just stick to the question "Who am I?" All other answers are just thoughts and thoughts can never be complete. Only silence is complete.

Quotes

"You cannot betray people unless you gain their trust. A wicked person first gains trust and then betrays. But even the deception of a wise man will only do the highest good."

"To be afraid of the wicked is a sign of a weak society and to be afraid to do bad is a sign of a strong society."

News Flash

B.R. Ambedkar Marathwada University has included the Art of Living Course in their curriculum. All those seeking higher education will get college credits by taking the course.

Twenty-five hard-core militants were totally transformed and they pledged to Guruji to drop violence.

Jai Guru Dev

SURRENDER

*T*he main impediment of many seekers on the path is that they want to surrender. Do not say that you want to surrender; know that you already are surrendered.

Wanting to surrender becomes an impediment on the path. This is like a child saying to its mother, "I want to love you." No child ever tells its mother, "I want to love you." Love is self-evident.

Surrender is not an act; it is a state of your being. Whether you acknowledge it or not, it is there. The wise wake up and see; the unwise take a longer time.

Know that you have no choice, you are in a state of surrender deep within you.

Anecdotes

A four-year-old child in an ART Excel meeting told Sri Sri, "I love you very much."

Sri Sri asked, "Why?"

She replied, "Because God has sneaked into your heart, and you are in God's heart."

In satsang, a man asked Sri Sri, "I do not feel the need for a Guru. What is your opinion of people like me?"

Sri Sri replied, with a twinkle in his eye, "Don't take my advice!" (*laughter*)

So, if he takes the advice, he has done what the master said and has become a disciple anyway! And if he does not take the advice, even then has he become a follower! It is a paradox.

News Flash
Enthusiastic devotees celebrated Holi, the festival of colors, with song, dance and laughter in the divine presence of the master in Rishikesh.

Our 5H program has benefited 1,050 villages in India in the first quarter alone.

The Gurumobile is on its way to Panchkula after a jubilant satsang in Chandigarh.

Jai Guru Dev

HOW TO HANDLE FEVERISHNESS

*W*hen you are in the grip of feverishness about
the result of your actions, what should you do?

Have faith and confidence that the result will be much
better than you can ever imagine. With faith you can
get rid of the feverishness of action and achievement.
Feverishness can also be a hangover from overactivity.
Then sleeping, listening to flute music, and bathing in
cold water can help.

Have dispassion. Know the whole thing will be over
one way or the other, and it does not matter.
Meditation and breathing can calm you down. Drop
whatever you are doing and do something completely
irrelevant. For example, while decorating your house,
take some time to mow the lawn or go shopping.
When you are doing something very important, take a
moment to do something totally irrelevant and
insignificant. This enhances your creativity. Relevant
action keeps you bound to the action. Irrelevant
action makes life a game.

News Flash

One of our devotees tricked two rival groups of hardcore terrorists and brought them to meet Guruji. Twenty-five of them belonged to one group, and the other 26 were their rivals. One meeting with the master and the transformation in them was total. The same people who had been responsible for chaos, disruption and killings in their state now took a vow to give up violence and to spread peace.

A jubilant Advanced Course with over 1,000 people concluded in Rishikesh yesterday.

Jai Guru Dev

HOW DOES A DESIRE ARISE?

1. A desire arises with the memory of a pleasant experience and past impressions.

2. A desire might arise through listening.

3. A desire can be triggered through association with certain people or a place.

4. Someone else's need or desire may manifest in you as your own desire, for example, when someone is hungry and you get a desire to feed them, or someone wants to talk with you and you get a spontaneous desire to talk with them.

5. Destiny or a happening in which you have a part to play may trigger a desire, but you are not aware of the reason for your actions. For example, a gentleman in Quebec, Canada kept making roads and working on a farm for 30 years, not knowing for what — the farm was destined to become our Montreal Ashram.

News Flash
*After a brief halt in Delhi, Guruji arrived in
Dharamshala as a state guest of the Government of
Himachal Pradesh, a picturesque place with temples,
snow-clad mountains and mango trees. His Holiness the
Dalai Lama warmly received Guruji at his residence and
had an hour-long meeting. Later he met all thirty Art of
Living teachers and devotees and lauded their
contribution to society. It was a treat to be in that
atmosphere of love, laughter and a total sense of
belongingness.*

*The second 5H Youth Training Program has begun in
Rishikesh with 240 participants. Of the planned 3,000
villages, work has already begun in 1,200.*

*Today is the Hindu New Year 5101 (52nd Century).
Happy New Year to all.*

Jai Guru Dev

RAM NAVAMI

Ra in Sanskrit means "that which is radiant" and *ma* means "myself."

That which shines forth within me is Rama. That which is radiant in every particle of the being is Rama.

Rama was born to Dasharatha and Kaushalya. Dasharatha means "the ten-charioted one" in Sanskrit. It signifies the five sense organs and the five organs of action. Kaushalya is Sanskrit for "skilled." The skillful driver of the ten chariots can give birth to Ram. When the five sense organs and the five organs of action are used skillfully, radiance is born within.

Rama was born in Ayodhya, which in Sanskrit means "the place where no war can happen." When there is no conflict in our mind, then radiance can dawn.

Lakshmana, the brother of Rama, was born of Sumitra - the good friend. When the ten are cooperating with you, awareness is born.

Often we try to look for radiance within. Just realize that you are radiant. Once when Sri Sri was 5 or 6 years old, he closed his eyes and said to a visiting saint, "Swamiji, I do not see any light." The saint replied, "You are the light! How can you see the light?"

News Flash
Vishu, the Tamil New Year, was celebrated with a grand pooja in the Bangalore Ashram.

Jai Guru Dev

DESIRE KILLS JOY AND ALL DESIRES AIM FOR JOY

*T*his couplet needs to be pondered over and over - a whole lifetime is not sufficient to digest this knowledge: desire kills joy and all desires aim for joy.

Whenever happiness has disappeared from your life, look deeper and you will see it is because of desire. And all that we desire is happiness!

No person, animal or creature desiring unhappiness is ever born; never has it happened before and never will it happen in the future.

When your small mind gets tired of running here and there, of wandering everywhere, it reaches the conclusion, "My desires have killed my happiness." A person who has conquered his desires is called "mahavira."

News Flash
Guruji had a satsang in Wayanad with over 12,000
people. Later he gave an address in a Catholic church on
Easter Sunday.

On his way back to Bangalore, Guruji addressed a
congregation organized by the Muslim League in Sultan
Batheri.

Jai Guru Dev

YOU ARE NOTHING

*E*ach experience completes. Completion means being led to void or nothing. In the progression of life, you will leave behind every experience saying, "This is nothing." Anything that is completed loses its importance. That is to say, it leads you to void - this is nothing.

A sign of intelligence is how soon you arrive at this understanding. Examine everything in life and say "This is nothing" and what remains is love, and that is everything.

When "This is nothing" does not come out of knowledge, it comes out of misery. Either through knowledge or through misery, you come to the point of "This is nothing, this is nothing." The choice is yours.

If you got this, it is really NOTHING. If you did not get this, never mind - this is nothing. *(laughter)*

News Flash
Guruji addressed the annual meeting of the
Confederation of Indian Industry in New Delhi and was
well received.

Guruji visited Ulaan Bataar, capital of Mongolia, on a
two-day state visit and was received by the first President
of the Mongolian Republic and a few members of
parliament. Though the flight was delayed by five hours,
thousands waited at the National Opera House, where
Guruji was driven straight from the airport. Even though
he had traveled such a long distance, there was not a
trace of tiredness as he greeted the cheering crowd. Guruji
tricked the security guards several times and mingled
with the crowd.

Meetings and satsangs at Ulaan Bataar were filled with
gratitude. A ten-year-old boy who was deaf for several
years regained his hearing! A lady who had suffered a
paralytic attack felt sensations all through her body on
seeing Guruji's picture in the newspapers. Three days
later, with some help, she came walking to attend
Guruji's satsang!

On April 29, Guruji was received by Mongolia's highest
Buddhist leader, His Holiness the Hamba Lama
Choijamts at the Gandan Monastery. The Lama, in his
welcome address, noted that Guruji's work has brought
much peace and strength to the people of Mongolia.

Jai Guru Dev

DESIRE FOR TRUTH

*B*uddha said that desire is the cause of all misery. If your desire does not get fulfilled, it leads to frustration and causes misery. Even if it does get fulfilled, it leaves you empty.

Vasishta said that desire is the cause of pleasure. You get pleasure from an object or a person only when you desire them. When you do not desire an object, you do not get pleasure from it. For example, when a person is hot and thirsty, a sip of cold water gives him pleasure; but there is no pleasure if he is not thirsty. Whatever gives you pleasure binds you and bondage is misery.

Sri Sri says when you desire truth, all other desires drop off. You always desire something that is not there. But truth is always there! Desire for truth removes all other desires; it dissolves and what remains is bliss.

News Flash
Teacher Training Courses ended on a celebrative note and with that began Guruji's South Asian tour. A well-attended live Kriya, followed by a satsang in a packed auditorium the next day, highlighted the Singapore visit.

A lady reporter asked Guruji how many followers he has, pointing to the people sitting in front of him. He replied, "I don't have any followers; they are all in front of me and I won't turn my back on anyone."

An Art of Living group presented the scientific research on mental health benefits of Sudarshan Kriya to the United Nation's Non-Governmental Organization Mental Health Committee. It was so well received that the discussion was extended an extra half hour.

Jai Guru Dev

SEEKERS BEWARE

*Y*ou can only seek that which you know and when you really do know, you already have it.

You cannot seek something you do not know.

Whatever you are seeking and wherever you seek, it is always only One; and the One is what you already are.

So, you cannot seek something you do not know and when you know what you are seeking, you already have it. When you seek the world, you get misery and when you want to find the way out of misery, you find the Divine.

A man lost a penny and was seeking it in a bush when he found a huge treasure. He was not seeking treasure but only for his lost penny. In the same way, when you seek something, you may get something else.

The truth, or Self, cannot be sought directly.

Dean: Many people come to the Art of Living seeking some mundane thing and find something else.
(*laughter*)

News Flash
Guruji's tour through Asia continued with nonstop
satsangs and celebrations with enthusiastic crowds in
Jakarta, Hong Kong and Taipei.

Guruji met with President Lee Teng-hui of the Republic
of China on Taiwan. The enthusiastic president started
talking about Art of Living activities to our own
delegation. He sought blessings for his people and his
continuing work on social programs.

Jai Guru Dev

IS THE GURU RESPONSIBLE?

*I*s the Guru responsible for your enlightenment?

If yes, and you do not get awakened, then the Guru is to be blamed. If you get freedom, then the Guru is also to be blamed because he has been partial to you. If the Guru could set you free, he could have done it to the whole world.

So the Guru is not responsible for your awakening. And yet freedom is next to impossible without the Guru. So the Guru is responsible and yet not responsible. This is a mystery.

News Flash
The police force in Slovenia is participating in an Advanced Course.

Reports of rural service projects are coming from all corners of India.

Jai Guru Dev

LIFE WITHOUT WISDOM IS INCOMPLETE

*W*isdom that does not give rise to feeling is incomplete.

Feeling that does not translate into action is incomplete.

Action that does not give rise to fulfillment is incomplete.

Fulfillment is returning to the Self.

News Flash
The Art of Living is actively involved in protecting the environment. About 80 full-grown 100-year-old trees were saved from illegal felling through the prompt action of the Art of Living. In North Gujarat, where thousands of cattle were dying of starvation and lack of water, the Art of Living has started a huge "Cattle Camp" to accommodate around 1,500 cattle.

Jai Guru Dev

EDUCATION

*E*ducation has five aspects:

1. Information - Often we think information is education, but it is only one aspect of education.

2. Concepts - Concepts are the basis for all research. You need to conceive in order to create.

3. Attitude - An integral aspect of education is cultivating the right attitude. Proper attitude at the right time and place determines your actions and behavior.

4. Imagination - Imagination is essential for creativity, for the arts. But if you get stuck in imagination, you can become psychotic.

5. Freedom - Freedom is your very nature. Only with freedom do joy, generosity and other human values blossom. Without freedom, attitudes become stifling, concepts become a burden, information is of no value and imagination becomes stagnant.

News Flash
Our volunteers have initiated a drought relief program in Gujarat. Cow Camps are on the way. This year the students in our rural school at Ved Vignan Mahavidyapeeth (VVM), Bangalore scored 100% on achievement tests.

Jai Guru Dev

TRUTH

*T*ruth is that which does not change. Examine your life and identify all that changes as not truth. With this outlook, you will find that you are surrounded by only untruth.

When you identify that which appears to you as untruth, then you will become free from it. When you do not identify the untruth, you cannot become free from it. Your own experiences in life make you identify your own untruth.

As you mature in life, you find everything is untruth - events, situations, people, emotions, thoughts, opinions, concepts, your body - everything is untruth. It is only then that satsang (the company of truth) happens in the real sense. For example, a mother cannot see the child as untruth until the child becomes an adult. For a baby, sweet is not untruth, and for a teenager, sex is not untruth.

Question: Is knowledge also untruth?

Sri Sri: Yes, if it is words, it is untruth. But as existence, it is truth. Love as an emotion is not truth; as existence, it is truth.

News Flash
After an enchanting satsang on a boat in Paris, Guruji has arrived for a brief and busy stay at the European Ashram in Bad Antogast, Germany.

The Art of Living in Shimla, India has undertaken a "Clean Shimla" project and a polyethylene bag-free city project.

Jai Guru Dev

I AM NEITHER HONEST NOR HUMBLE

A lady: I want an honest and humble man in my life.

Sri Sri: I am neither honest nor humble. (*Everyone is shocked*.) I cannot tell everyone I am God, as not everyone will understand. So I am not honest. I am not humble - how can God be humble?

If I am humble, I am not honest.
If I am honest, I cannot be humble! (*laughter*)

Hide your dispassion and express your love. By expressing dispassion you lose enthusiasm in life. And by not expressing love you feel stifled. Expressing dispassion may bring ego. Hide dispassion in your heart like the roots of a tree and express love like a ripe fruit.

News Flash
Guruji had given perfume to Mr. Salim, a devotee from
Kollam. He called back to say that though he sprayed
the perfume on many people, to everyone's amazement
the bottle stayed full.

Jai Guru Dev

How To Deal With Humiliation

*K*now that humiliation does not weaken you - it strengthens you.

When you have a sense of belongingness, you do not feel humiliated. The more egotistic you are, the more humiliation you feel. When you are childlike and have a greater sense of kinship, then you do not feel humiliated.

When you are committed to truth and not to your ego, then you also do not feel humiliated.

If you are afraid of humiliation, you can neither make progress in your material life nor in your spiritual life.

When you stand above humiliation, you get closer to the Self - to God. When you are steeped in love, with the Existence, with the Divine, nothing whatsoever can humiliate you.

So the way out of humiliation is:
    Get humiliated.
    Be childlike.
    Be crazy.
    Get steeped in love with the Divine.
    Totally commit yourself to truth, to knowledge.

News Flash
There was an Advanced Course of 115 people and a Teacher Training Course with 70 people at the Bakal Ashram in Siberia. Divya Samaj Nirman (DSN) - Creating a Divine Society - Courses in Europe are keeping everyone on a high.

As people poured into the Montreal Ashram to join Guruji for the summer programs, there was no space left, not even for the mosquitoes.

Jai Guru Dev

LEGENDS

*L*egendary is the love that withstands rejection. It will be free of anger and ego.

Legendary is the commitment that withstands humiliation. It will be one-pointed and will reach the goal.

Legendary is the wisdom that withstands turbulence. It will be integrated into life.

Legendary is the faith that withstands a million chances of doubt. It will bring perfection (siddhis).

Legendary are the events that withstand time. They will become morals for the millions.

News Flash
The first Art of Living Basic Course was held in Bangladesh.

Jai Guru Dev

Arguments And Wrong Action

A person who argues should not be given knowledge. An argumentative mind is not receptive to knowledge. When someone is in an argumentative mood, then giving knowledge or advice is in vain. In an argumentative mood you feel you know it all. Then you are not ready for knowledge. That is why wise people do not give advice when they are in an argumentative environment.

Argument has a purpose. It can bring out the truth if there is no emotion or sense of "I" attached to it. Argument can also have a disadvantage. It can make untruth appear to be truth.

A wise man will not take arguments seriously; he will just have fun with them. Wisdom is beyond all arguments.

Both a worldly person and a spiritual person will tell you not to do wrong, though the reasons they give are totally different. A worldly person will tell you not to do wrong because it hurts or causes him pain. A spiritual person will tell you not to do wrong because it would only harm you more.

Exercise
Identify any one specific virtue or good quality you would like to have. Ask for it on Guru Purnima day (the full moon - July 15-16) and know that you have it.

News Flash
Guruji received the highest commendation from the mayor's office of the city of San Francisco for his contributions to society and for the indelible impression he has left on the community of San Francisco and the world.

Jai Guru Dev

VIRTUES

*V*irtues cannot be cultivated. You have to assume that they are there.

In the Gita, Krishna said to Arjuna, "Grieve not Arjuna, you are born with virtues."

The seeker should remember that he is born with virtues; otherwise he could not have been a seeker.

If you think you do not have virtues and then try to cultivate them, you will fail.

You often compare yourself with others on the basis of virtues. Do not compare yourself with them. Simply recognize all the virtues you appreciate in others, and realize that they are already present in you in seed form. You only have to nurture them.

When you think you do not have a virtue, then you come from a space of lack or deficiency.

Caroline: Aho! That is why we don't need positive affirmations!

Alice: Affirmations really don't work anyway.

Sri Sri: Affirmations do not work because you think you do not have those virtues, and with affirmation you try to have them.

And so Caroline affirms: You are the home of all virtues. (*laughter*)

News Flash
The Guru Purnima celebrations started with the divine sound of the Guru Puja being chanted by hundreds of devotees from all over the world who traveled here to be in the presence of their beloved master. The next evening, all gathered around Guruji for a cruise to the middle of Lake Tahoe for a celebration of music and sweet silent meditation as the full moon rose over the surrounding peaks of the Sierra Nevada Mountains of eastern Kapillaranya (California).

Jai Guru Dev

The Art of Living Foundation

The *Art of Living Foundation* is devoted to making your life a celebration. A nonprofit educational organization run by volunteers, we offer workshops for self-development and spiritual growth that allow busy people to take maximum advantage of Sri Sri Ravi Shankar's multidimensional teachings. We are officially accredited as a Non-Governmental Organization (NGO) with the United Nations, and we sponsor service projects worldwide, including programs for people living with HIV and cancer, rehabilitative training for prisoners and vocational training for rural people in Asia.

Our *Dollar-a-Day* program provides children with food, clothing and schooling. Founded in 1981 and accredited as a charitable nonprofit institution, *Ved Vignan Mahavidyapeeth* (Institute of Vedic Science) provides many essential educational and medical services. The Institute has grown to house and serve boys and girls from 22 surrounding villages. All services are administered, at no charge, to each child through funding from supporting individuals and groups.

The *5-H Program* is a joint effort of the *International Association of Human Values (IAHV)* and Ved Vignan Mahavidyapeeth. The 5-H Program offers social and community development projects with a focus on Health, Hygiene, Homes, Harmony in Diversity and Human Values. This unique and comprehensive approach involves training at-risk youth to become community leaders. IAHV's *Homes for Change* program is building homes, wells and septic systems for poor families in India.

One successful organization using our techniques for a special purpose is the *Prison SMART* (Stress Management and Rehabilitative Training) Foundation, which is licensed to teach a variation of our Art of Living Basic Course in correctional facilities and juvenile detention centers in the United States. Their programs are innovative and solution-oriented.

The *Art of Living Basic Course* is the ideal introduction to Sri Sri's wisdom. This 16-18 hour program over 6 days has uplifted the lives of thousands. Breath contains the secret of life. Breath is linked to the vital life energy in us - prana. Low prana translates into depression, lethargy, dullness and poor enthusiasm. When the mind and body are charged with prana, we feel alert, energetic and joyful. Specific breathing techniques can revitalize and invigorate our physical and emotional well-being. One learns several powerful breathing practices, including Sudarshan Kriya, a unique process that fully oxygenates the cells, recharging them with new energy and life. Negative emotions stored as toxins in the body are naturally flushed out. Tension, anger, anxiety, depression and lethargy are released and forgotten. The mind is left calm and centered, with a clearer vision of the world, our relationships and ourselves. The heart of the workshop also includes processes and deep insights into the nature of life and how to be happy. To take this workshop contact the Art of Living Center nearest you. See the directory on page 110.

Art of Living Advanced Courses are specially designed for those who have completed the Basic Course. These retreats spent in silence provide you a profound opportunity to explore the depths of your own inner silence through deep meditation, enjoyable processes and seva (service). Each evening ends with a celebration of singing, dancing and wisdom. You leave feeling renewed emotionally and elevated spiritually, with a dynamism for greater success in all your activities. Some Advanced Courses are offered in Sri Sri's presence - meeting the master personally is the experience of a lifetime.

Sahaj Samadhi Meditation. Not one of us lacks spiritual depth. The peace and happiness we feverishly seek in the world are already contained within us, covered only by the clouds of stress and strain. These clouds are lifted with Sahaj Samadhi meditation, a gift of wisdom from Sri Sri. Sahaj Samadhi meditation provides a rest much deeper than sleep. Like awakening renewed on a sunny morning, your outlook on life becomes realigned toward the positive. Stress drops off, the chattering mind becomes serene and creative, aging slows and you rediscover the unshakable contentment of your inner Self. Sahaj Samadhi meditation is easy to learn and practice. With simple guidance, anyone can meditate. Personal instruction is offered at Art of Living Centers worldwide.

Our course for children and teens, the *ART Excel* Course, All 'Round Training for Excellence, provides practical techniques that enable young people to handle negative emotions such as fear, anger and frustration in positive ways. The ART Excel Course also teaches vital non-academic skills such as the art of making friends, the secret of popularity, and the value of service to others - all in a supportive, yet challenging and fun atmosphere. Our toughest critics - the kids themselves - give this program rave reviews.

You can visit our web site at: www.artofliving.org

Art of Living Books and Tapes

Books, videotapes, and audiotapes of Sri Sri are available by mail. Titles include: God Loves Fun, The Path of Love, Compassion and Trust, The Purpose of Life, The Ultimate Relationship, Om Shanti Shanti Shanti and the Yoga Sutras of Patanjali.

For a catalog of products and to order, contact:

Art of Living Books and Tapes
(800) 574-3001 U.S.A. or (641) 472-9892
Facsimile: (641) 472-0671
E-mail: aolmailorder@lisco.com

Worldwide Art of Living Centers

For more information about Art of Living courses,
workshops, and programs, contact a center closest to you:

AFRICA
Hema & Rajaraman
Art of Living
P.O. Box 1213
Peba Close Plot 5612
Gaborone, Botswana
Tel. 26-735-2175
Aolbot@global.co.za

CANADA
Art of Living Foundation
P.O. Box 170
13 Infinity Rd.
Saint-Mathieu-du-Parc
Quebec G0X 1N0
Canada
Tel. (819) 532-3328
artofliving.northamerica@
sympatico.ca

GERMANY
Akadamie Bad Antogast
Bad Antogast 1
77728 Oppenau
Germany
Tel. 49-7804-910-923
Artofliving.Germany@
t-online.de

INDIA
Vyakti Vikas Kendra, India
No. 19, 39th A Cross,
11th Main
4th T Block, Jayanagar
Bangalore 560041, India
Tel. 91-80-6645106
vvm@vsnl.com

UNITED STATES
Art of Living Foundation
P.O. Box 50003
Santa Barbara, CA 93150
Tel. 805-564-1002
U.S. toll free: 877-399-1008
www.artofliving.org